Laughter Never Gets Old

Text by
Bob Phillips

Artwork by
JONNY HAWKINS

HARVEST HOUSE PUBLISHERS
EUGENE, OREGON

Cover by Dugan Design Group, Bloomington, Minnesota

LAUGHTER NEVER GETS OLD

Copyright © 2015 Artwork by Jonny Hawkins; Text by Bob Phillips
Published by Harvest House Publishers
Eugene, Oregon 97402
www.harvesthousepublishers.com

ISBN 978-0-7369-5894-3 (pbk.)

Printed in the United States of America

15 16 17 18 19 20 21 22 23 / BP-JH / 10 9 8 7 6 5 4 3 2 1

To everyone who loves cartoons and humor

We are especially grateful for those creative and humorous individuals who come up with unique and funny thoughts and anonymously share them through the Internet for all to enjoy. We would happily acknowledge you by name if we knew who you were. Thank you for the smiles you bring to our faces.

You're Getting Older When...

- Almost everything hurts, and what doesn't hurt doesn't work.

- The gleam in your eyes is from the sun hitting your bifocals.

- It feels like the morning after, but you didn't go anywhere last night.

- Your little black book contains only names ending in MD.

- Your children look middle-aged.

- You finally reach the top of the ladder and realize it's leaning against the wrong wall.

- Your mind makes contracts your body can't meet.

- A dripping faucet triggers an uncontrollable bladder urge.

- You look forward to a dull evening.

- Your favorite part of the newspaper is "20 Years Ago Today."

- You turn out the lights for economic reasons rather than romantic ones.

- You sit in a rocking chair but can't get it going.

- Your knees buckle, but your belt won't.

- You regret all those mistakes you made by resisting temptations.

- You're 17 inches around the neck, 42 inches around the waist, and 96 around the golf course.

- Your back goes out more often than you do.

- A fortune-teller offers to read your face.

- Every time you see a pretty girl pass by your window, your pacemaker opens the garage door.

- The little old gray-haired lady you help across the street is your wife.

- You sink your teeth into a steak, and they stay there.

- You have too much room in the house but not enough in the medicine cabinet.

- You get your exercise acting as pallbearer for your friends who exercise.

- You know all the answers, but nobody asks you the questions.

◇◇◇

I'm having Alzheimer's, amnesia, and déjà vu at the same time. I think I've forgotten this before.

◇◇◇

I find the older I get, the better I used to be.

◇◇◇

"Still on that high fiber diet, hon?"

New Diet Rules

1. If you eat something and no one sees you eat it, it has no calories.

2. If you drink a diet soda with a candy bar, the calories in the candy bar are canceled out by the diet soda.

3. When you eat with someone, the calories don't count if you don't eat more than he or she does.

4. In foods used for medicinal purposes, such as hot chocolate, pancakes, and Sara Lee cheesecake, the calories never count.

5. If you fatten up everyone else around you, you will look thinner.

6. In movie-related items, such as Milk Duds, buttered popcorn, Junior Mints, Red Hots, and Tootsie Rolls, the calories don't count because you eat them in the dark.

7. Cookie pieces contain no calories. The process of breaking causes calorie leakage.

8. When you are preparing something to eat, stuff licked off knives and spoons has no calories.

9. Foods of the same color—such as spinach and pistachio ice cream—have the same number of calories.

10. Chocolate is a universal color and may be substituted for any other food color.

11. When on vacation, any foods eaten above 5000 feet do not contain calories. You can eat to your heart's content. But take caution when returning home. (Caution: Below 5000 feet, some kind of expansion may take place.)

◇◇◇

The man who is a pessimist before 48 knows too much; if he is an optimist after it, he knows too little.

—*Mark Twain*

◇◇◇

I was listening to some rap music this afternoon. Not that I had a choice—it was coming out of a Jeep four miles away.

—*Nick DePaulo*

◇◇◇

Q: What's the best way to keep a youthful figure?
A: Ask a woman her age.

◇◇◇

Son: Mommy, why do you have some gray hairs?
Mother: Well, son, every time you disobey, I get a new strand of gray hair.
Son: Oh, so *that's* why Grandma's hair is all gray.

◇◇◇

You know you've caught the computer virus when you wake up at three in morning to go to the bathroom, and on the way back you stop and check your e-mail.

◇◇◇

Bill: I always have a valet park my car.
Sam: Why's that?
Bill: He's more likely to remember where he put it.

◇◇◇

Reporter: I understand you've turned 93 and have a lot of great-grandchildren.
Grandmother: Actually, I expect they're all pretty ordinary.

◇◇◇

Eleanor: I do wish George would stop biting his nails. It's such a horrible habit.
Ruth: My Hubert did the same thing. But I found a way to stop him.
Eleanor: How did you do that?
Ruth: I hid his teeth!

◇◇◇

"Don't try the fruitcake yet, Harold,
until it stiffens."

Obituary

Please join me in remembering a great icon of the entertainment community—the Pillsbury Doughboy, who died of a yeast infection and trauma complications from repeated pokes in the belly. He was 71.

Doughboy was buried in a lightly greased coffin. Dozens of celebrities turned out to pay their respects, including Mrs. Butterworth, Hungry Jack, the California Raisins, Betty Crocker, the Hostess Twinkies, and Captain Crunch. The grave was piled high with flours.

Aunt Jemima delivered the eulogy and lovingly described Doughboy as a man who never knew how much he was kneaded. Doughboy rose quickly in show business, but his later life was filled with turnovers. He was considered a very smart cookie but wasted much of his dough on half-baked schemes. Though sometimes a little flaky and a bit of a crusty old man, he was considered a positive roll model for millions.

Doughboy is survived by his wife, Play-Doh; by four children—John Dough, Jane Dough, Do Si Dough, and one in the oven—and by his elderly father, Pop Tart.

The funeral was held at 3:50 for about 20 minutes.

The family invites you to share this information with anyone who may be having a crumby day and kneads a lift.

◇◇◇

"…And senior citizens need only give 9%."

Good News and Bad News for Your Pastor

Good news—you baptized seven people today in the river.

Bad news—you lost two of them in the current.

Good news—the women's guild voted to send you a get-well card.

Bad news—it passed 31 to 30.

Good news—the elder board accepted your job description the way you wrote it.

Bad news—they were so inspired by it, they also formed a search committee to find somebody capable of filling the position.

Good news—you finally found a choir director who approaches things the same way you do.

Bad news—everyone in the choir quit.

Good news—Mrs. Jones is wild about your sermons.

Bad news—Mrs. Jones was also wild about *The Gong Show*, *The Three Stooges*, and *The Texas Chain Saw Massacre*.

Good news—the trustees finally voted to add more church parking.

Bad news—they decided to pave the front lawn of the parsonage.

Good news—church attendance rose dramatically the last three weeks.
Bad news—you were on vacation.

Good news—your biggest critic just moved away.
Bad news—he is now your bishop.

Good news—the youth group is coming to your house for a surprise visit.
Bad news—it's the middle of the night, and they're armed with toilet paper and shaving cream.

◇◇◇

One day a man was visiting Sea World in San Diego, California. He looked at the various attractions but became tired of walking around. He decided to rest on a bench by a pond that was filled with large carp. He was about to sit down when a little boy almost slipped into the pond. The quick-thinking man grabbed the boy's arm just in time to keep him from getting wet. Unfortunately, as the man was saving the young lad, his wallet slipped out of his pocket and fell into the water.

Before the man could retrieve his wallet, a hungry carp snatched it up. As the fish started to swim away, a larger carp grabbed the wallet from the first fish. Soon all the fish were engaged in a big fight for the wallet.

The man thought to himself, "I'll never be able to get it back with all of this carp-to-carp walleting."

◇◇◇

The older you get, the fewer things seem worth waiting in line for.

◇◇◇

You can tell you're growing older when you spend a lot of time thinking about the thermostat.

◇◇◇

You can tell you're getting older when your doctor informs you that your blood type has been discontinued.

◇◇◇

Q: What's the worst thing about growing older?
A: Having to listen to the advice of your children.

◇◇◇

You can tell you're getting older when you fall asleep and someone wakes you to make sure you're not dead.

◇◇◇

You can tell you're getting older when people compliment your alligator shoes even though you're barefoot.

◇◇◇

"My Grandma did the cutest thing
the other day…"

How Old Is Grandpa?

One evening a boy was talking to his grandfather about current events. He asked his grandfather what he thought about the shootings at schools, the computer age, and just things in general.

The granddad replied, "Well, let me think a minute. I was born before television, photocopiers, contact lenses, Frisbees, and the pill.

"We didn't have radar, credit cards, laser beams, or ball-point pens.

"Man had not invented panty hose, air conditioners, dishwashers, or clothes dryers. Man hadn't orbited the earth, let alone walked on the moon.

"Your grandmother and I got married first and then lived together. Most every family had a father and a mother.

"Until I was 25, I called every man older than me 'sir,' and after I turned 25, I still called police officers and every man with a title 'sir.' I was born before gay rights, computer dating, dual careers, daycare centers, and group therapy.

"Our lives were governed by the Ten Commandments, good judgment, and common sense. We were taught to know the difference between right and wrong and to stand up and take responsibility for our actions.

"Serving our country was a privilege, and living here was an even bigger privilege.

"We thought fast food was what people ate during Lent.

"Having a meaningful relationship meant getting along with your cousins.

"'Time-sharing' meant spending time with the family in the evenings and weekends, not purchasing condominiums.

"We never heard of FM radios, CDs or DVDs, yogurt, or guys wearing earrings.

"We listened to big bands, Jack Benny, and the president's speeches on our radios.

"The term 'making out' referred to how you did on your school exam.

"Pizza Hut, McDonalds, Chick-fil-A, and instant coffee were unheard of.

"We had five and dime stores, where we could actually buy things for five and ten cents.

"Ice-cream cones, phone calls, rides on a streetcar, and Pepsi were all a nickel. And if we didn't want to splurge, we could spend that nickel on enough stamps to mail a letter or two postcards.

"We could buy a new Chevy coupe for $600, but who could afford one? Too bad, because gas was only 11 cents a gallon.

"In my day, grass was mowed, Coke was a cold drink, pot was something your mother cooked in, and rock music was your grandmother's lullaby. Aids were helpers in the principal's office, a chip was a piece of wood, hardware was found in a hardware store, and 'software' wasn't even a word.

"No wonder people call us old and confused. You might even say we have a generation gap."

◇◇◇

"Still getting feedback from your hearing aid?"

Crying over Math

Last week I purchased a burger at a fast-food restaurant for $1.58. I gave the cashier two dollars, and a moment later I pulled eight cents from my pocket and gave it to her. She stood there, holding the nickel and three pennies while looking at the screen on her register.

I sensed her discomfort and tried to tell her to just give me two quarters, but she hailed the manager for help. He tried to explain the transaction to her, but she started to cry.

Why do I tell you this? Because of the evolution in teaching math since the 1950s.

Teaching math in 1950. A logger sells a truckload of lumber for $100. His cost of production is four-fifths of the price. What is his profit?

Teaching math in 1960. A logger sells a truckload of lumber for $100. His cost of production is four-fifths of the price, or $80. What is his profit?

Teaching math in 1970. A logger sells a truckload of lumber for $100. His cost of production is $80. Did he make a profit?

Teaching math in 1980. A logger sells a truckload of lumber for $100. His cost of production is $80, and his profit is $20. Your assignment—underline the number 20.

Teaching math in 1990. A logger cuts down a beautiful forest because he is selfish and inconsiderate and cares nothing for the habitat of animals or the preservation of our woodlands. He does this so he can make a profit of $20! What do you think of this way of making a living? Discussion question—How did the birds and squirrels feel as the logger cut down their homes? (There are no wrong answers, and if you feel like crying, it's okay.)

Teaching math in 2000. Who cares? Just steal the lumber from your rich neighbor. He won't have a gun to stop you. Redistribute the wealth to those less fortunate.

Teaching math in 2010. Don't worry about that greedy logger and his business. His $20 profit will be taxed so much that he can't even afford a $5 hamburger.

◇◇◇

You know you're getting older when the happy hour is a nap.

◇◇◇

Age is a quality of mind.
If you've left your dreams behind,
If hope is cold,
If you no longer look ahead,
If your ambitions' fires are dead—
Then you are old.

But if from life you take the best,
And if in life you keep the jest,
If love you hold;
No matter how the years go by,
No matter how the birthdays fly—
You are not old.

◇◇◇

"How ya doin', old timer?"

Should I Join Facebook?

When I bought my BlackBerry, I thought about the 30-year business I ran with 1800 employees. I did it without a cell phone that plays music, takes pictures and videos, and communicates with Facebook and Twitter. Under duress, I signed up for Twitter and Facebook so my seven kids, their spouses, my thirteen grandkids, and my two great-grandkids could communicate with me in a modern way. I figured I could handle something as simple as Twitter with only 140 characters of space.

That was before one of my grandkids hooked me up for Tweeter, Tweetree, Twhirl, Twitterfon, Tweetie, and Twittererific, Tweetdeck, Twitpix and something that sends every message from every other texting program to my cell phone. My phone was beeping every three minutes with the details of everything except the bowel movements of the entire next generation. I'm not ready to live like this. I now keep my phone in the garage in my golf bag.

The kids bought me a GPS for my last birthday because they say I get lost every now and then going to the grocery store or library. I kept that in a box under my workbench with the Bluetooth (it's red) phone I'm supposed to use when I drive. I wore the Bluetooth device once while standing in line at Barnes & Noble, talking to my wife. Everyone within 50 yards was glaring at me. I had to take my hearing aid out to use it, and evidently I got a little loud.

The GPS looked pretty smart on my dashboard, but the lady inside that gadget was the most annoying, rudest person I had run into in a long time. Every ten minutes, she sarcastically said, "Re-calc-u-lat-ing." You would think she could be nicer. She sounded as if she could barely tolerate me. She would let go with a deep sigh and then tell me to make a U-turn at the next light. Then if I made a right turn instead, well, it was not a good relationship.

When I get really lost now, I call my wife and tell her the name of the cross streets. She is starting to develop the same tone as Gypsy the GPS Lady, but at least she loves me.

To be perfectly frank, I'm still trying to learn how to use the cordless phones in our house. We've had them for years, but I still haven't figured out how I can lose three phones all at once and have to run around digging under chair cushions and checking bathrooms and the dirty laundry baskets when the phone rings.

The world is just getting too complex for me—even when I go to the grocery store. You would think the checkers could make a simple decision, but this sudden "Paper or plastic?" every time I check out just knocks me for a loop. I bought some of those cloth reusable bags to avoid looking confused, but I never remember to take them with me.

Now I toss it back to them. When they ask me, "Paper or plastic," I just say, "Doesn't matter to me. I'm bi-sacksual." Then it's their turn to stare at me with a blank look.

I was recently asked if I tweet. I answered, No, but I do toot a lot."

—author unknown

◇◇◇

"You asked me if I Twittered."

You know you're getting older when you light your last candle on the cake and the first one has already burned out.

◇◇◇

A very wealthy old man had been virtually deaf for years until he was finally given a new type of hearing aid implant. For the first time he could hear perfectly.

"Your family must be really pleased that you can hear again," his doctor said.

"I haven't told them yet," the old man replied. "I just sit around and listen to their conversations. I've changed my will three times in the last month!"

◇◇◇

Strange Thoughts

- If the police arrest a mime, do they tell him he has the right to remain silent?

- Why do the signs saying "Slow Children" have a picture of children running?

- How does the highway department get deer to cross the road only at those yellow road signs?

- Do mortuaries give lifetime guarantees for their coffins?

- When hams are cured, what disease did they have?

- If space is a vacuum, where do the bags come from, and who changes them?
- What was the best thing before sliced bread?
- Can atheists get insurance for acts of God?
- Do egotists talk about other people?
- When a block of cheese has its picture taken, what does it say?
- Is it possible to cry underwater?
- If practice makes perfect and nobody's perfect, why practice?
- What will happen if you get scared half to death twice?
- How can you tell when you run out of invisible ink?
- Who designed a square box for a round pizza?
- Do chickens think rubber humans are funny?
- Does the little mermaid wear an algebra?
- Do people in Australia call the rest of the world "up over"?
- How is it possible to have a civil war?
- Why is it that your nose runs and your feet smell?

- If one synchronized swimmer drowns, do the rest drown too?

- Before people used drawing boards, what did they go back to?

- Will you get a ticket for driving in the car-pool lane on the freeway if you are driving a hearse with a corpse in it?

- What do you plant to grow a seedless watermelon?

- If you ate both pasta and antipasto, would you still be hungry?

- If a tin whistle is made of tin, what is a fog horn made of?

◇◇◇

A group of pensioners in the lounge of a nursing home were exchanging complaints about their ailments.

"My arms are so weak I can hardly hold this cup."

"My cataracts are so bad I can't even see to pour my coffee."

"I can't turn my head because of the arthritis in my neck."

"My blood pressure pills make me feel dizzy all the time."

"I guess that's the price we pay for getting old."

Finally, one of the group spoke up. "I know we all have a lot of complaints, but I think we should talk about something positive."

A little old man to the side of the group raised his hand. "I know something we can all be grateful for. We can still drive."

◇◇◇

There are three stages to man—the first 30 years he learns, the next 30 years he earns, and the next 30 years he yearns.

◇◇◇

Q: Do people sleep more soundly as they age?
A: Yes, but it's usually in the afternoon.

◇◇◇

Three elderly men with impaired hearing were walking down the street one blustery day in March.

One said, "Windy, ain't it?"

"No," said the second, "it's Thursday."

The third man said, "So am I. Let's go have a Coke."

◇◇◇

Put the Seniors in Jail

Let's put the seniors in jail and the criminals in a nursing home.

This way the seniors would have access to showers, hobbies, and walks. They would receive unlimited free prescriptions, dental and medical treatment, and wheelchairs. And they'd receive money instead of paying it out.

They would have constant video monitoring, so they could be helped instantly if they fell or needed assistance. Bedding would be washed twice a week, and their clothes would be ironed and returned to them.

A guard would check on them every 20 minutes and bring meals and snacks to their cells. They would have family visits in a suite built for that purpose. They would have access to a library, a weight room, spiritual counseling, a pool table, and education.

Simple clothing, shoes, slippers, PJs, and legal aid would be available on request and free. Private rooms would be provided for all, as well as an outdoor exercise yard with gardens. Each senior could have a computer, a TV, a radio, and daily phone calls. A board of directors would hear complaints, and guards would strictly adhere to a code of conduct.

The criminals, in turn, would get cold food. They would be left alone and unsupervised and would take showers once a week. Lights would be off at eight p.m. They would live in a tiny room, pay $5000 per month, and have no hope of ever getting out.

Finally, there would be justice for all.

◇◇◇

"Yay—I just won a Grammy!"

We Love America

Some of us are walking a little slower these days, and our eyes and ears are not what they once were.

We have worked hard, raised our children, worshipped our God, and grown old together. Yes, we are the ones some refer to as being over the hill, and that is probably true. But before you write us off completely, you should take a few things into consideration.

In school we studied English, history, math, and science, which enabled us to lead America into the technological age.

Most of us remember what outhouses were—many of us with firsthand experience. We remember the days of telephone party lines, 25-cent gasoline, and milk and ice being delivered to our homes. A few of us even remember starting cars with a crank. Yes, we lived those days.

Many people consider us old-fashioned and outdated. But we won World War II and fought in Korea and Vietnam. We can quote the Pledge of Allegiance, and we know where to place our hand while doing so.

We wore different uniforms but carried the same flag. We know the words to "The Star Spangled Banner," "America," and "America the Beautiful" by heart. You may even see some tears running down our cheeks as we sing.

We feel no obligation to apologize to anyone for America.

—*author unknown*

◇◇◇

I'm the Life of the Party

- I'm the life of the party—I just can't remember where I'm at.

- I'm good at opening childproof caps—with a hammer.

- I'm awake many hours before my body allows me to get up.

- I smile all the time because I can't hear a thing you're saying.

- I'm sure everything I can't find is in a safe and secure place—somewhere.

- I'm wrinkled, saggy, lumpy—and that's just my left leg.

- I'm beginning to realize that aging is not for wimps.

- I'm a walking storeroom of facts—I've just lost the key to the storeroom door.

- I've got a photographic memory—I'm just out of film.

◇◇◇

You can tell you're getting older when your birthday suit needs pressing.

◇◇◇

Grampoline

A 95-year-old man was asked, "What is the formula for such a long life?"

He replied, "Just keep breathing."

◇◇◇

At least when you become a senior citizen you know that all of your personal secrets are safe with your friends. They can't remember them either.

◇◇◇

You know you're getting older when your talk centers on abbreviations like SS, IRA, and AARP.

◇◇◇

A truck driver stopped to help a lady change a tire in a downpour. As he finished the job, soaked to the skin, he banged the hubcap into place.

"Shh," said the woman. "You'll wake my husband. He's asleep in the backseat."

◇◇◇

No wonder we can't display the Ten Commandments in a courthouse or Congress. Posting "Thou shalt not steal," "Thou shalt not commit adultery," and "Thou shalt not lie" in buildings full of lawyers, judges, and politicians would create a hostile work environment.

◇◇◇

Things My Children Taught Me

1. If you spray hair spray on dust bunnies and run over them with roller blades, they can ignite.

2. A three-year-old's voice is louder than 200 adults in a crowded restaurant.

3. You should not toss baseballs up when the ceiling fan is on.

4. A ceiling fan can hit a baseball a long way.

5. The glass in a window (even a double-pane window) doesn't stop a baseball hit by a ceiling fan.

6. When you hear the toilet flush and someone say "Uh-oh," it's already too late.

7. Brake fluid mixed with Clorox makes smoke—and lots of it.

8. A king-size water bed holds enough water to fill a 2000-square-foot house with four inches of water.

9. "Play-Doh" and "microwave" should never be used in the same sentence.

10. VCRs do not eject peanut butter and jelly sandwiches regardless of what kids see on TV commercials.

11. Marbles in gas tanks make lots of noise when driving.

12. Always look in the oven before you turn it on.

13. Plastic toys do not like ovens.

14. The spin cycle on the washing machine does not make earthworms dizzy.

15. However, the spin cycle does make cats dizzy.

16. Cats throw up twice their body weight when dizzy.

◇◇◇

A Harley rider is cruising by the National Zoo in Washington, DC, when he sees a little girl leaning into the lion's cage. Suddenly, the lion grabs her by the collar of her jacket and tries to pull her inside to slaughter her right in front of her screaming parents.

The biker jumps off his Harley, runs to the cage, and lands a powerful punch square on the lion's nose. Whimpering in pain, the lion jumps back, letting go of the girl. The biker carries her to her terrified parents, who thank him endlessly.

A reporter witnessed the whole event. The reporter came up to the biker and said, "That was the most gallant and bravest action I've ever seen!"

The Harley rider replied, "It was nothing, really. The lion was behind bars. I just saw this little kid in danger and acted as I felt right."

The reporter said, "Well, I'll make sure this doesn't go unnoticed. I'm a journalist, and tomorrow's paper will have this story on the front page. What do you do for a living? What political affiliations do you have?"

The biker replied, "I'm a United States Marine and a Republican."

The journalist scribbled some notes and left.

The following morning the biker bought a paper to see if his story was there. There it was on the front page in big letters:

"US Marine assaults African immigrant and steals his lunch."

◇◇◇

Be nice to your kids. They'll be choosing your nursing home.

◇◇◇

Husband: Do old men wear boxers or briefs?
Wife: Depends.

◇◇◇

"Never too old to rock and roll."

I'm a Senior Citizen

- I'm the life of the party—even if it lasts until 8:30.

- I'm usually interested in going home before I get to where I am going.

- I'm very good at telling stories—over and over and over.

- I'm aware that other people's grandchildren aren't as cute as mine.

- I'm well cared for—eye care, dental care, arthritis care, long-term care...

- I'm sure everything I can't find is in a safe place somewhere.

- I'm a walking storeroom of facts, but I've lost the key to the storeroom door.

- I'm having trouble remembering simple words like...

◇◇◇

You can tell you're getting older when you go to a restaurant and your server asks for your money up front.

◇◇◇

An older gentleman was driving on a freeway when he received a frantic phone call from his wife.

"George, I just saw on the news that someone is driving on the freeway in the wrong direction. Look out for him!"

Driving with one hand and holding the cell phone with the other, George responded, "I think they made a mistake. It's not just one car driving the wrong way—there are hundreds of them!"

◇◇◇

A reporter asked a man who was celebrating his hundredth birthday, "What's the secret of your long life?"

"My motto throughout life has been to avoid arguments at all costs. I never argue with anyone."

The reporter was a little skeptical. "There must be some other reason—exercise, natural remedies, diet…I can't believe you have lived to be a hundred simply by not arguing!"

The old man said, "You know, you could be right."

◇◇◇

"I just want him to be able to
see what he's wearing."

New Laws

The law of preemptive knowledge: It's better to know it and not need it than it is to need it and not know it.

The law of reciprocity: Customers don't care how valuable they are to you. They only care how valuable you are to them.

The law of unsuccessful employees: One cannot do what he is told, and the other cannot do anything unless he is told.

The law of exploration: The greatest underdeveloped territory in the world lies under your hat.

The law of service: Good service can save a bad meal. A good meal cannot save bad service.

The law of computing: Artificial intelligence is no match for natural stupidity.

The law of leniency: Favors granted always become defined as rights.

The law of statistics: The rate of unemployment is 100 percent if you're the one who is unemployed.

The law of excuses: If you do it, it's done.

The law of hierarchy: If you're at the top of the ladder, cover your backside. If you're at the bottom, cover your face.

The law of convergence: If two people are in a kitchen, they will head for the same spot sooner rather than later.

The law of history lessons: The further back you look, the further forward you can see.

◇◇◇

Signs of the Times

On a college bulletin board: "Books for sale—like new, hardly used."

In a podiatrist's office: "Time wounds all heels."

On a septic tank truck: "Yesterday's Meals on Wheels"

On a sales lot for mobile homes: "Wheel Estate"

On a reducing salon: "Thinner Sanctum"

In an allergist's office: "Wheeze be seated."

On a plumber's truck: "We repair what your husband fixed."

On another plumber's truck: "Don't sleep with a drip. Call your plumber."

In an obstetrician's office: "Pay as you grow."

On a watch repair shop: "Come in and see us when you haven't got the time."

On a clock repair shop: "Cuckoo clocks psychoanalyzed here."

In a science-fiction bookstore: "Shoplifters will be disintegrated."

On a tire shop: "Invite us to your next blowout."

On an electrician's truck: "Let us remove your shorts."

In a nonsmoking area: "Smoking won't send you to hell…it just makes you smell as if you've been there."

On maternity room door: "Push. Push. Push."

At an optometrist's office: "If you don't see what you're looking for, you've come to the right place."

In a taxidermist's window: "We really know our stuff."

On a fence: "Salesmen welcome! Dog food is expensive!"

At a car dealership: "The best way to get back on your feet—miss a car payment."

Outside a muffler shop: "No appointment necessary. We hear you coming."

In a veterinarian's waiting room: "Be back in five minutes. Sit. Stay."

At the electric company: "We will be delighted if you send in your payment. However, if you don't, you will be."

In a restaurant window: "Don't stand there and be hungry—come on in and get fed up."

In the front yard of a funeral home: "Drive carefully. We'll wait."

At a propane filling station: "Thank heaven for little grills."

On church bulletin boards:

> "We have a prophet sharing plan for you."
>
> "Seven days without God makes one weak."
>
> "You think it's hot today!"
>
> "Free trip to heaven. Details inside."
>
> "Try our Sundays. They're better than Baskin-Robbins."
>
> "Soul food served here."
>
> "Don't give up. Moses was once a basket case."

"Under the same management for nearly 2000 years."

"The wages of sin are not likely to be reduced."

◇◇◇

Have you heard of the new steak house called Elvis Presley's Famous Steaks? It is designed to appeal to diners who love meat tender.

◇◇◇

Mahatma Gandhi walked barefoot, which produced a huge set of calluses on his feet. He ate very little, which made him frail, and with his odd diet, he suffered from bad breath. This made him a super calloused fragile mystic hexed by halitosis.

◇◇◇

A teacher wanted to teach some math concepts to his students. Since it was near Halloween, he decided to use a pumpkin as an illustration. He asked the students, "What do you get if you divide the circumference of a pumpkin by its diameter? Everyone was silent until one boy raised his hand.

"Yes, Johnny, what's your answer?"

"You get pumpkin pi."

◇◇◇

Did you hear about the man whose dentures were rotting away? He asked his dentist, "Why is this happening to me? These dentures are falling apart, and they're less than a year old."

The dentist examined him and said, "The problem is, you've eaten too much hollandaise sauce. The acidity in the sauce corrodes your dentures. I'm going to have to make you a brand-new plate made out of chrome."

The man was a little surprised and asked, "Why out of chrome?"

The dentist replied, "Because there's no plate like chrome for the hollandaise."

◇◇◇

An older couple was lying in bed one morning. They had just awakened from a good night's sleep. But when the man took his wife's hand, she said, "Don't touch me"

"Why not?" he asked.

She answered, "Because I'm dead!"

"What are you talking about?" said the husband. "We're lying here in bed together and talking to one another!"

"No, I'm definitely dead."

He insisted, "You are not dead. What in the world makes you think you're dead?"

"I woke up this morning and nothing hurts."

◇◇◇

"My husband is a World War II vet.
He doesn't *go* to the beach, he *storms* it."

Senior Citizens Are Not to Blame

Senior citizens are not the ones who took…

the melody out of music,

the pride out of appearance,

the courtesy out of driving,

the romance out of love,

the commitment out of marriage,

the responsibility out of parenthood,

the togetherness out of the family,

the learning out of education,

the service out of patriotism,

the Golden Rule from rulers,

the Nativity scene out of cities,

the civility out of behavior,

the refinement out of language,

the dedication out of employment,

the prudence out of spending,

the ambition out of achievement,

or God out of government and schools.

◇◇◇

Nine Words Women Use

1. *Fine.* This is the word women use to end an argument when they are right and you need to shut up.

2. *Five minutes.* If she is getting dressed, this means a half an hour. If you are watching the game before helping around the house, it means five minutes.

3. *Nothing.* This is the calm before the storm. This means something, and you should be on your toes. Arguments that begin with *nothing* usually end in *fine*.

4. *Go ahead.* This is a dare, not permission. Don't do it!

5. *Loud sigh.* This isn't actually a word, but it's a nonverbal statement men often misunderstand. A loud sigh means she thinks you are an idiot and wonders why she is wasting her time arguing with you about *nothing*. (See number 3.)

6. *That's okay.* This is one of the most dangerous statements a woman can make to a man. It means she wants to think long and hard before deciding how and when you will pay for your mistake.

7. *Thanks.* A woman is thanking you. Do not question her or faint. Just say, "You're welcome."

8. *Whatever*. This is a woman's way of saying shut up…now!

9. *Don't worry about it; I got it*. Another dangerous statement. A woman has told a man several times to do something, but she is now doing it herself. This will later result in a man asking, "What's wrong?" For the woman's response, refer to number 3.

◇◇◇

Minister: We are gathered together at this funeral to pay final homage to a good man. He was a kind man, a man whom everyone loved, a man who treasured his family as his family treasured him.

Mother: Waldo, go up and make sure it's Grandpa in that coffin.

◇◇◇

An elderly couple passed away as a result of a car accident. Upon their arrival in heaven, Saint Peter showed them around. It was fantastic. They felt great and had plenty to eat, the weather was just right, and swimming pools and tennis courts were everywhere. Finally the husband leaned over to his wife and said, "Gertrude, we could have been here ten years ago if you hadn't heard about all them fancy low-fat diets."

◇◇◇

Church Bulletin Bloopers

- The third verse of "Blessed Assurance" will be sung without musical accomplishment.

- The low self-esteem support group will meet Wednesday from 7:00 to 8:00 p.m. Please use the back door.

- Reverend Cookingham spoke briefly, much to the delight of the audience.

- The Harris family will attend the funeral of Becky's former husband, who died in Denver, Colorado, tomorrow.

- The annual potluck supper is next Sunday. Prayer and medication will follow afterward.

- Don't let worry kill you off. Let the church help.

- Tonight's sermon will be gin at 6 p.m.

◇◇◇

You've entered the golden years when the silver in your hair turns to lead in your pants.

◇◇◇

You can tell you're getting older when you stop lying about your age and start bragging about it.

◇◇◇

Did you hear about the funeral for the guy who invented the hokey-pokey? First, they put his left leg in...

◇◇◇

Scoutmaster: Well, boys, did you do your good deeds for the day?
First scout: Yes, sir. We helped an elderly lady cross the street.
Scoutmaster: It took both of you?
Second scout: Yes, sir. She didn't want to go.

◇◇◇

Texting for Seniors

More and more seniors are texting and tweeting, so there appears to be a need for an STC (Senior Texting Code). If you qualify for senior discounts, this is the code for you. Be sure to pass this on to your children and grandchildren so they can understand your texts.

ADT......... At the doctor's

BFF .... Best friend fainted

BTW .... Bring the wheelchair

BYOT .... Bring your own teeth

CBM .... Covered by Medicare

CGU .... Can't get up

CUATSC..... See you at the senior center

DWI . . . . Driving while incontinent

FWBB . . . . Friend with beta blockers

FWIW . . . . Forgot where I was

FYI . . . . Found your insulin

GGPBL . . . . . . Gotta go, pacemaker battery low

GHA . . . . Got heartburn again

FWIPMK. . . . . Forgot where I put my keys

HGBM . . . . . . Had good bowel movement

IMHO . . . . Is my hearing aid on

LMDO. . . . . . . Laughing my dentures out

LOL . . . . Living on Lipitor

LWO . . . . Lawrence Welk's on

OMMR . . . . . . On my massage recliner

ROFL,CGU. . . Rolling on floor laughing,
                     can't get up

TTYL. . . . . Talk to you louder

WAITT . . . . . . Who am I talking to

WAP. . . . . Where are prunes?

WWNO. . . . . . Walker wheels need oil

◇◇◇

You're never too old to learn—unless, of course, you're a teenager.

◇◇◇

First older gentleman: How did you convince that beautiful 23-year-old girl to marry you when you were 73?

Second older gentleman: I told her I was 90.

◇◇◇

First older gentleman: My minister told me, "You know, you're not getting any younger. You need to start thinking about the hereafter."

Second older gentleman: What did you say to him?

First older gentleman: I said, "I'm already doing that at least five times a day. Every time I go into another room to get something, I ask myself, 'What am I here after?'"

◇◇◇

Far-Out Thoughts

- Do not argue with an idiot. He will drag you down to his level and beat you with experience.

- Light travels faster than sound. This is why some people appear bright until you hear them speak.

- If I agreed with you, we'd both be wrong.

- War doesn't determine who is right—only who is left.

- Knowledge is identifying a tomato as a fruit. Wisdom is not putting it in a fruit salad.

- Evening news begins with "Good evening" and proceeds to tell you it isn't.

- Women will never be equal to men until they can walk down the street with a bald head and a beer gut and still think they are sexy.

- Money can't buy happiness, but it sure makes misery easier to live with.

- I used to be indecisive. Now I'm not sure.

- You're never too old to learn something stupid.

- Nostalgia isn't what it used to be.

- Change is inevitable—except from a vending machine

- Where there's a will, there are relatives.

- You don't need a parachute to skydive. You only need it to skydive twice.

◇◇◇

A man and his wife were having an argument about who should brew the coffee each morning.

The wife said, "You should do it because you get up first. And then we won't have to wait as long to get our coffee."

The husband said, "You're the cook around here. You should do it because that's your job. I can just wait for my coffee."

The wife replied, "No, you should do it. Besides, the Bible says the man should make the coffee."

The man started laughing. "I can't believe that. Show me."

The wife fetched the Bible, opened the New Testament, and showed him the top of several pages, where it indeed says "Hebrews."

◇◇◇

Reporter: Now that you're 90 years old, to what do you attribute your good health?

Elderly man: I'm not sure yet. I'm still negotiating with a mattress company and two breakfast-food firms.

◇◇◇

He's so old, he can remember when AT&T was just called "A."

◇◇◇

To All the Smart People

What do the seven words listed below have in common? No fair peeking at the answer. See if you can discover the solution first. It's not that they all have at least two double letters.

1. banana
2. dresser
3. grammar
4. potato
5. revive
6. uneven
7. assess*

◇◇◇

People say you'll lose your mind when you grow older. What they don't tell you is that you won't miss it very much.

—*Malcolm Cowley*

◇◇◇

Experience is a wonderful thing. It enables you to recognize other people's mistakes. You can't live long enough to make them all yourself. Trust me—I've tried!

◇◇◇

---

* *Answer*: In all of the words listed, if you take the first letter, place it at the end of the word, and then spell the word backward, it will be the same word.

Observations on Growing Older

- Your kids are becoming you—and you don't like them. But your grandchildren are perfect.

- Going out is good. Coming home is better.

- You forget names, but it's okay because other people forget they even knew you.

- Your spouse is counting on you to remember things you don't remember.

- You no longer care to do the things you used to do, but you really do care that you don't care to do them anymore.

- Your husband sleeps better on a lounge chair with the TV blaring than he does in bed. It's called "pre-sleep."

- You miss the days when everything worked with just an On and Off switch.

- You tend to use four-letter words more often: "What?" "When?"

- Your freckles have become liver spots.

- Everybody whispers.

- Now that your husband has retired, you'd give anything if he'd find a job.

- You have three sizes of clothes in your closet—two of which you will never wear again.

◇◇◇

"Zantac…Prilosec…Rolaids…
Get your antacids here!"

You know you're getting older when people no longer view you as a hypochondriac.

◇◇◇

A psychological study in 1995 found that three minutes spent looking at a fashion magazine caused 70 percent of women to feel depressed, guilty, and shameful.

◇◇◇

The good news about being middle-aged is that the glass is still half full. The bad news is that pretty soon your teeth will be floating in it.

◇◇◇

Grandfather: Did you know that Abraham Lincoln said, "You can fool some of the people all of the time, and all of the people some of the time"?
Grandson: Well, what happens the rest of the time?
Grandfather: I reckon they're likely to make fools of themselves.

◇◇◇

They don't make mirrors the way they used to. The ones I buy now are full of wrinkles.
—*Phyllis Diller*

◇◇◇

Middle age is when the broadness of the mind and the narrowness of the waist change places.

◇◇◇

Bizarre Thoughts

1. If you try to fail and succeed, which have you done?

2. If a stealth bomber crashes in a forest, does it make a noise?

3. Do cemetery workers prefer the graveyard shift?

4. Why is it called tourist season if we can't shoot them?

5. Why do they call it lipstick if you can still move your lips?

6. How does the guy who drives the snowplow get to work?

7. Why aren't airplanes made of the same indestructible material used to make the little black box?

8. How do you know if a dictionary misspelled a word?

9. If nothing sticks to Teflon, how does Teflon stick to the pan?

10. If all the world's a stage, where does the audience sit?

11. Why do "slow up" and "slow down" mean the same thing?

12. Why don't sheep shrink when it rains?

13. Why can't women apply mascara with their mouths closed?

14. Why is "abbreviation" such a long word?

15. If someone has a midlife crisis while playing hide-and-seek, does he automatically lose because he can't find himself?

16. Why do they wait until a pig is dead to cure it?

17. Why does the sun darken our skin but lighten our hair?

18. If we are here on earth to help others, what are the others here for?

◇◇◇

"Grandma, your reading glasses don't work—
I *still* can't read."

First wife: Where can a man in his seventies find a
    younger and pretty woman who would be inter-
    ested in him?
Second wife: In the library.
First wife: In the library?
Second wife: In the fiction section.

◇◇◇

Noah's Ark
Everything I need to know, I learned from Noah's ark.

- Don't miss the boat.
- Plan ahead. It wasn't raining when Noah
  built the ark.
- Stay fit. When you're 60 years old, someone
  may ask you to do something really big.
- Don't listen to critics; just get on with the
  job that needs to be done.
- Build your future on high ground.
- For safety's sake, travel in pairs.
- Speed isn't always an advantage. The snails
  were on board with the cheetahs.
- When you're stressed, float awhile.
- Remember, the ark was built by amateurs,
  the Titanic by professionals.

◇◇◇

An 80-year-old couple was having problems remembering things, so they decided to go to their doctor to get checked out to make sure nothing was wrong with them. When they arrived, they explained to the doctor about the problems they were having with their memory. After checking the couple out, the doctor told them they were physically okay but might want to start writing things down and making notes to help them remember things.

Later that night while watching TV, the old man got up from his chair. His wife asked, "Where are you going?"

"I'm going to the kitchen."

"Will you get me a bowl of ice cream?"

"Sure."

"Do you think you should write it down so you can remember it?" she asked.

"No, I can remember that," he replied.

"I'd like some strawberries on top," she said. "You better write that down 'cause I know you'll forget that."

"I can remember that. You want a bowl of ice cream with strawberries."

"I'd also like some whipped cream on top," she said. "I know you'll forget that, so you better write it down."

He started to feel irritated. "I don't need to write that down. I can remember that."

About 20 minutes later, he returned from the kitchen and handed her a plate of bacon and eggs. She stared at the plate for a moment and said, "You forgot my toast."

◇◇◇

Daffy Dictionary

abash: a great party

abdicate: to give up all hope of ever having a flat stomach

absentee: a missing golf peg

acoustic: a long pole used to play pool

acre: someone with aches and pains

administer: increasing the clergy

adult: someone who has stopped growing at both ends and started growing in the middle

alarms: what an octopus is

announce: one sixteenth of a pound

antique: an item your grandparents purchased, your parents threw away, and you purchased

archive: where Noah kept his bees

autopsy: a dying practice

bagels: birds that live near a bay

balderdash: a rapidly receding hairline

bank: a place where you can borrow money (provided you can prove you don't need to)

barium: what doctors do when the treatment fails

belittle: the imperative form of "shrink"

benign: what you be after you be eight

bounty hunter: seeker of paper towels

burglarize: what some crooks see with

bush pilot: someone who flew Air Force One

calendar: something that goes in one year and
out the other

Camelot: where to shop for a dromedary

carpe diem: gripe of the day

catalyst: several cats' names written in alpha-
betical order

cistern: opposite of brethren

class action: a stylish deed

clothes dryer: an appliance that eats socks

coffee: a person who is coughed upon

college professor: someone who talks in other
people's sleep

condescend: a prisoner climbing down a wall

damnation: the country of beavers

daze: opposite of knights

dermatologist: one who makes rash judgments

detail: remove an animal's hind extremity

diet: a short period of starvation followed by a
gain of five pounds

dilate: to live long

donation: a country of female deer

dreadlocks: the fear of opening the dead bolt

egotist: someone who is usually me-deep in
conversation

electrician: someone who wires for more
money

enlist: n, n, n, n, n

experience: the name men give to their
mistakes

eye dropper: a clumsy ophthalmologist

fad: something that goes in one era and out the
other

fibula: a small lie

flabbergasted: appalled by how much weight
one has gained

forfeit: what most animals stand on

Girl Scout: a young male looking for young
females

glutton: someone who eats the slice of cake
you wanted

gossip: letting the chat out of the bag

gross ignorance: 144 times worse than ordinary
ignorance

groundhog: sausage

handicap: ready-to-use hat

handkerchief: cold storage

hanging: a suspended sentence

hate crime: who doesn't?

hernia: pertaining to the female knee

heroes: what a guy in a boat does

hypochondriac: someone who won't leave well enough alone

impeccable: unable to be eaten by a chicken

infantry: a sapling

inpatient: where the lost scalpel can be found

Internet scam: dot con

iota: a Toyota with payments still due

justice: a decision in your favor

kangaroo: spiritual advisor for metal food containers

ketchup: what slow runners are always trying to do

laughingstock: cattle, horses, sheep, and hogs responding to a really good joke

liability: a talent for fibbing

life jacket: a coat that will last a lifetime

light-year: a year with fewer calories

liver: one who isn't dead

locomotive: crazy reason

lute: money

lymph: walks with a lisp

malpractice: shopping until you get it right

maritime: hour when the wedding will start

masseurs: people who knead people

May: a month when you might

meanderthal: a wandering caveman

"You're sure you want
your kitchen tiled in these?"

megaphone: a very large telephone

Milk Dud: a dairy cow that won't produce

monologue: a conversation between a politician and somebody else

moonlighting: the sun's other job

morbid: a higher offer

neighborhood: a felon who lives near you

node: past tense of know

obesity: surplus gone to waist

octopus: eight-legged cat

old-timer: one who remembers when the moon inspired romance, not space travel

ostracized: the same size as an ostrich

outpatient: a person who has fainted

oxymoron: as dumb as an ox

pharmacist: a helper on a farm

plankton: 2000 pounds of lumber

polarize: what penguins see with

polite: a lamp on a pole

polygon: a dead parrot

postoperative: a letter carrier

practical nurse: a nurse who marries a wealthy patient

praise: let off esteem

primate: remove your spouse from in front of the television

"Those aren't smoke rings.
That's his dog breath."

profound: an expert discovered

quarterback: change when buying a 75-cent item with a dollar bill

rectum: nearly killed 'em

remind: a brain transplant

remote control: (female) a device for changing the channel on the television

remote control: (male) a device that scans 175 channels in less than five minutes

repartee: what a person thinks of after he becomes a departee

resolve: an admirable quality in ourselves or detestable stubbornness in others

ringworm: worm with a bell

security: what guards drink

seizure: a roman emperor with epilepsy

selfish: what the seafood store sells

shortening: one of the important ingredients in a good sermon

silverfish: a fish slightly less expensive than a goldfish

sonogram: a telegram from your son

stagnation: a country of single men

sweater: a person who freely perspires

sweet 16: just down the hall from suite 14

tact: changing the subject without changing your mind

"I can't mow the lawn—
I have rider's block."

tangent: a man who's been in the sun

tax: a fine for doing fine

tea: break fluid

terminal illness: airport sickness

thesaurus: a dinosaur that knows a lot of words

timekeeper: person who didn't return your watch

tireless: having a car but no wheels

toothache: pain that drives you to extraction

ultrasound: any very loud noise

unabated: a fishhook without a worm

untold wealth: what you left out on April 15

varicose: nearby

vein: conceited

walnut: one who is mad about climbing vertical barriers

warehouse: what you ask when you are lost

weak-kneed: seven days of preparing dough for bread

wholesale: where a gopher goes to buy a home

writer: one who corrects a wrong

yawn: an honest opinion openly expressed

yoke: Swedish humor

◇◇◇

First wife: Does your husband have any trouble with memory storage?

Second wife: No, not at all. His problem is with retrieval.

◇◇◇

You can tell you're getting older when the doctor no longer takes X-rays but just holds you up to the light.

◇◇◇

A 75-year-old woman in a retirement home was admiring a 90-year-old man.

"Why do you keep looking at me so much?" asked the man.

"Well," she responded, "you look just like my third husband."

"How many husbands have you had?"

"Two."

◇◇◇

A grandfather was speaking to his children, grandchildren, and great grandchildren. "Don't think of me as an old man. I'm as healthy as a horse. Everything is fine. My heart's still pumping away, my liver is strong, and my mind, knock on wood…Who is it?"

◇◇◇

"Oh, hi Bernie—we were just talking
about the good old days."

The Old Paths

I liked the old paths, when
Moms were at home,
Dads were at work,
Brothers went into the army,
And sisters got married before having children.

Crime did not pay,
Hard work did,
And people knew the difference.

Moms could cook,
Dads would work,
And children would behave.

Husbands were loving,
Wives were supportive,
And children were polite.

Women wore the jewelry,
And men wore the pants.
Women looked like ladies,
Men looked like gentlemen,
And children looked decent.

People loved the truth
And hated a lie.
They came to church to get in,
Not to get out.

Hymns sounded godly,
Sermons sounded helpful,

Rejoicing sounded normal,
And crying sounded sincere.

Cursing was wicked,
Drugs were for illness,
And divorce was unthinkable.

The flag was honored,
America was beautiful,
And God was welcome.

We read the Bible in public,
Prayed in school,
And preached from house to house.

To be called an American was worth dying for,
To be called a Christian was worth living for,
To be called a traitor was a shame.

Preachers preached because they had a message,
And Christians rejoiced because they had the victory.
Preachers preached from the Bible,
Singers sang from the heart,
And sinners turned to the Lord to be saved.

A new birth meant a new life,
Salvation meant a changed life,
And following Christ led to eternal life.

Being a preacher meant you proclaimed the
    Word of God,
Being a deacon meant you served the Lord,
Being a Christian meant you lived for Jesus,

And being a sinner meant someone was praying
  for you.

Laws were based on the Bible,
Homes read the Bible,
And churches taught the Bible.

God was worshipped,
Christ was exalted,
And the Holy Spirit was respected.

Church was where you found Christians
On the Lord's Day, rather than in the garden,
On the creek bank, on the golf course,
Or being entertained somewhere else.

—author unknown

◇◇◇

Vice President Joe Biden went to visit an adult care facility to cheer up the residents. However, he was disappointed and dismayed that none of the older folks recognized him. They just quietly looked at him. Finally, he went up to one of the older women and said, "Do you know who I am?"

The elderly woman responded, "No, I don't know. But if you'll wait just a minute, I'll go get one of the nurses. I'm sure they can tell you who you are."

◇◇◇

"And remember, His eye is on the sparrow and
He nose all you snowbirds."

An Obituary for Common Sense

Today we mourn the passing of a beloved old friend, Common Sense, who has been with us for many years. No one knows how old he was because his birth records were lost long ago in bureaucratic red tape. He will be remembered as having learned many valuable lessons:

- come in out of the rain
- the early bird gets the worm
- life isn't always fair
- sometimes it's my fault

Common Sense lived by simple, sound financial policies (don't spend more than you earn) and reliable strategies (adults, not children, are in charge).

His health began to deteriorate rapidly when well-intentioned but overbearing regulations were set in place. Reports of a six-year-old boy charged with sexual harassment for kissing a classmate, teens suspended from school for using mouthwash after lunch, and a teacher fired for reprimanding an unruly student only worsened his condition.

Common Sense lost ground when parents attacked teachers for doing the job they themselves had failed to do in disciplining their unruly children. His health declined even further when schools were required to get parental consent to administer sunscreen or an aspirin to a student but could not inform parents when a student became pregnant and wanted to have an abortion.

Common Sense lost the will to live as churches became businesses and criminals received better treatment than their victims. Common Sense took a beating when people couldn't defend themselves from burglars in their own homes and the burglars could sue them for assault.

Common Sense finally gave up the will to live after a woman failed to realize that a steaming cup of coffee was hot. She spilled a little in her lap and was promptly awarded a huge settlement.

Common Sense was preceded in death by his parents, Truth and Trust, by his wife, Discretion, by his daughter, Responsibility, and his son, Reason. He is survived by his four stepbrothers—I Know My Rights, I Want It Now, Someone Else Is to Blame, and I'm a Victim.

His funeral was not well attended because so few realized he was gone.

◇◇◇

Doctor: Mr. Erickson, you are in good health. You
    should live to be 90.
Mr. Erickson: I'm 91!
Doctor: See, what did I tell you?

◇◇◇

You can tell you're getting older when you lose your breath playing checkers.

◇◇◇

"This is where my grandma goes to seed."

One of the great things about growing older is that the things you buy won't wear out.

⟡⟡⟡

You know you've caught the computer bug when you find yourself e-mailing your buddy whose desk is right next to yours.

⟡⟡⟡

When I was younger, I was taught to respect my elders. Now I have a big problem. I don't have anyone to respect.

⟡⟡⟡

No wonder computers can do more work than people. They don't have to stop and answer the phone.

⟡⟡⟡

I had a friend who was a clown. When he died, all his friends went to the funeral in one car.

—*Steven Wright*

⟡⟡⟡

"Grandma, how can I put one of your hugs
in my scrapbook?"

What I Learned from My Mother

My mother taught me how to become an adult: "If you don't eat your vegetables, you'll never grow up."

My mother taught me wisdom: "When you get to be my age, you'll understand."

My mother taught me ESP: "Put on a sweater. You're cold."

My mother taught me medical science: "If you keep crossing your eyes, they'll freeze that way."

My mother taught me religion: "You'd better pray that comes out of the carpet!"

My mother taught me to think ahead: "If you don't pass your spelling test, you'll never get a good job."

My mother taught me logic: "Because I said so, that's why."

My mother taught me to meet a challenge: "What were you thinking? Answer me when I talk to you. And don't you dare talk back to me!"

My mother taught me irony: "Keep crying and I'll give you something to really cry about!"

My mother taught me humor: "When that lawn mower cuts off your toes, don't come running to me."

My mother taught me genetics: "You're just like your father."

My mother taught me about my roots: "Do you think you were born in a barn?"

My mother taught me about anticipation: "Just wait until your father gets home."

My mother taught me about receiving: "Boy you're going to get it when we get home."

My mother taught me about justice: "When you grow up and have kids, I hope you have one just like you. Then you'll see what it's like."

◇◇◇

A man in India could drop into a deep trance in less than three minutes. He earned a lot of money from people who wanted to learn his secret.

One day this man had a terrible toothache and had to go to a dentist. The dentist informed him that he would have to use Novocain to deaden the area in order to perform a root canal. The man refused the Novocain and said that he would rather use transcend dental medication.

◇◇◇

A hotel in Los Angeles was jam-packed with chess players from all over the United States who had gathered for the national chess championship.

A group of the players surrounded a fireplace in the lobby. Pretty soon the players became very loud as they talked about their victories over other players. Someone who was staying at the same hotel but was not a chess player became irritated by all the noise. He went to the manager of the hotel and said, "I can't stand these chess nuts boasting in an open foyer."

◇◇◇

Q: What's the difference between a clown and a man having a midlife crisis?

A: The clown knows he's wearing ridiculous clothes.

◇◇◇

The seven ages of a man are spills, drills, thrills, bills, ills, pills, and wills.

◇◇◇

Being 102 years old has its benefits—no peer pressure.

◇◇◇

At a fancy party, an attractive matron asked a young man to guess her age. "You must have some idea," she said as he hesitated.

"I have several ideas," he admitted with a smile. "The trouble is, I can't decide whether to make you ten years younger on account of your looks or ten years older on account of your charm."

◇◇◇

Little Suzie: "My grandmother is always complaining about how terrible it feels to be old."

Little Janie: "Mine too. I guess those wrinkles hurt a lot."

◇◇◇

"That's funny…I don't remember
our children getting married."

Forgetful?

Just a line to say I'm living,
That I'm not among the dead,
Though I'm getting more forgetful
And more mixed in the head.
For sometimes I can't remember,
When I stand at foot of stair,
If I must go up for something
Or I've just come down from there.

And before the fridge, so often,
My poor mind is filled with doubt.
Have I just put food away
Or come to take some out?

And sometimes when it is dark out,
And my nightcap's on my head,
I don't know if I'm retiring
Or just getting out of bed.

So if it's my turn to write you,
There's no need getting sore.
I may think that I have written
And don't want to be a bore.

So remember—I do love you,
And I wish that you were here.
But now it's nearly mail time,
So I must say, "Goodbye, dear."

There I stood beside the mailbox
With a face so very red.
Instead of mailing you my letter,
I had opened it instead.

—author unknown

◇◇◇

I'm not old. I'm chronologically gifted!

◇◇◇

Retired people don't mind being called senior citizens when they get the 10 percent discount.

◇◇◇

An old man was concerned that his wife was losing her hearing. He wanted to check to see if what he had been thinking was true. One evening while she was cooking in the kitchen, he quietly snuck up behind her and said softly, "Honey, what's for dinner?"

There was no response. He moved a little closer and again said, "Honey, what's for dinner?"

There was still no response. He moved even closer and said, "Honey, what's for dinner?"

Finally, she turned around with a disgusted look on her face and said, "For the third time, I told you it was chicken!"

◇◇◇

"He used to kiss me and I'd see fireworks.
Now all I see are flared nostrils."

Classy Insults

Lady Astor: "If you were my husband I'd poison your tea."

Winston Churchill: "If you were my wife, I'd drink it."

Walter Kerr: "He had delusions of adequacy."

Winston Churchill: "He has all the virtues I dislike and none of the vices I admire."

Clarence Darrow: "I have never killed a man, but I have read many obituaries with great pleasure."

Moses Hadas: "Thank you for sending me a copy of your book. I'll waste no time reading it."

Stephen Bishop: "I feel so miserable without you. It's almost like having you here."

Mark Twain: "I didn't attend the funeral, but I sent a nice letter saying I approved of it."

George Bernard Shaw: "I am enclosing two tickets to the first night of my new play. Bring a friend if you have one."

Winston Churchill: "Cannot possibly attend first night. Will attend second if there is one."

John Bright: "He is a self-made man and worships his creator."

Irvin S. Cobb: "I've just learned about his illness. Let's hope it's nothing trivial."

Samuel Johnson: "He is not only dull himself, he is the cause of dullness in others."

Paul Keating: "He is simply a shiver looking for a spine to run up."

Forrest Tucker: "He loves nature in spite of what it did to him."

◇◇◇

You can tell you're getting older when your ears are hairier than your head.

◇◇◇

You're getting older if you can remember when the Dead Sea was only sick.

◇◇◇

You know you're getting older when you try to blow out the candles on your birthday cake and the heat from the flames drives you back.

◇◇◇

Comfort food

The Top Ten Reasons We Are Overweight

10. With hundreds of channels of great television 24 hours a day, who has time to exercise?

9. Girl Scout Cookies get better every year.

8. The colossal failure of the Salad King drive-thru franchise.

7. Just to spite Richard Simmons.

6. Adding a diet soda to your bacon cheeseburger with chili fries to make it a healthy meal.

5. It's not really butter.

4. Fashion models are not good examples of real American women for our little girls.

3. Slimfast tastes better with a scoop of Ben & Jerry's.

2. Sprinkles!

1. Did somebody say McDonalds?

◇◇◇

Doctor: Mr. West, I'm afraid you are dying.
Patient: How long have I got?
Doctor: Ten…
Patient: Ten what? Ten months, ten weeks, ten days?
Doctor: …nine, eight, seven, six…

◇◇◇

The Ten Commandments, Redneck Style

1. Just one God.
2. Nothin' before God.
3. Watch yer mouth.
4. Git yourself to Sunday meeting.
5. Honor yer ma and pa.
6. No killin'.
7. No foolin' around with another fella's gal.
8. Don't take what ain't yers.
9. No telling tales or gossipin'.
10. Don't be hankerin' for yer buddy's stuff.

◇◇◇

A man will laugh at a woman trying to put on eye makeup, yet he will take ten minutes trying to make three hairs look like six.

◇◇◇

After my thirtieth birthday, instead of growing hair on my head, I started growing it in places where I didn't need it, like the top of my ear. A strand sprouted there overnight and made me look like something out of *The Cat in the Hat.*

—*Bill Cosby*

◇◇◇

Bumper Snickers

- I used to be a schizophrenic, but we're okay now.

- Energizer Bunny arrested, charged with battery.

- Do not wash—this vehicle is undergoing a scientific dirt test.

- You're just jealous because the voices only talk to me.

- My dog Mitten swallowed a shuttlecock—bad Mitten.

- Everyone is entitled to my opinion.

- Never, never, never, repeat yourself.

- I brake for hallucinations.

- Always remember, you're unique—just like everyone else.

- I doubt, therefore I might be.

- A balanced diet is a cookie in both hands.

- My mother was a travel agent for guilt trips.

- I is a college student.

- Stop repeat offenders—don't reelect them.

- Conserve trees. Eat a beaver.

- I tried to daydream, but my mind kept wandering.

- Caution! Driver applying makeup.

- Go ahead and hit me. I need the money.
- Five out of four people have trouble with fractions.
- I don't suffer from insanity—I enjoy every minute of it.
- Wear short sleeves—support your right to bare arms.
- Cleverly disguised as a responsible adult.
- We're not old people, we're recycled teenagers.
- Today is the day for decisive action. Or is it?
- Madness takes its toll. Please have exact change.

◇◇◇

First mother: My children are driving me crazy.

Second mother: But children are a great comfort in old age.

First mother: That may be true, but they help you reach it faster than you want to!

◇◇◇